Unix & Linux
Shell Scripting Tutorial

(c) 2000 – 2017 Steve Parker

Version:2.0e

A Bourne Shell Programming/Scripting Tutorial for learning about using the Unix shell.

- Join in on Facebook, at http://facebook.com/shellscript

- Check out the *nixShell Blog at http://nixshell.wordpress.com/

- Follow Hints and Tips at https://www.shellscript.sh/tips/

- See this book's Amazon page at http://amzn.com/dp/B00C2EGNSA

Table of Contents

1. Introduction

Purpose Of This Tutorial

This tutorial is written to help people understand some of the basics of shell script programming, and hopefully to introduce some of the possibilities of simple but powerful programming available under the bourne shell. As such, it has been written as a basis for one-on-one or group tutorials and exercises, and as a reference for subsequent use.

A Brief History of sh

Steve Bourne wrote the Bourne shell which appeared in the Seventh Edition Bell Labs Research version of Unix. Many other shells have been written; this particular tutorial concentrates on the Bourne and the Bourne Again shells. Other shells include the Korn Shell (ksh), the C Shell (csh), and variations such as tcsh. This tutorial does *not* cover those shells.

Audience

This tutorial assumes some prior experience; namely:

* **Use** of an **interactive** Unix shell
* **Minimal programming knowledge** - use of variables, functions, is useful background knowledge

- Understanding of **some** Unix/Linux commands, and **competence** in using **some** of the **more common** ones.
- Programmers of **ruby, perl, python, C, Pascal**, or any programming language (even BASIC) who can maybe read shell scripts, but don't feel they understand exactly how they work.

Typographical Conventions Used in This Tutorial

Significant words will be written in *italics* when mentioned for the first time. Code segments and script output will be displayed as monospaced text. Command-line entries will be preceded by the Dollar sign ($). If your prompt is different, enter the command:

```
PS1="$ "
```

Then your interactions should match the examples given (such as $ ./my-script.sh below). Script output (such as "Hello World" below) is displayed at the start of the line.

Text that is to be entered by you, is shown in **bold text**.

```
$ echo '#!/bin/sh' > my-script.sh
$ echo 'echo Hello World' >> my-script.sh
$ chmod 755 my-script.sh
$ ./my-script.sh
Hello World
$
```

Entire scripts will include a reference to where the plain text of the script may be downloaded, where available (links will be from https://www.shellscript.sh/eg/)

Shell Scripting Tutorial

first.sh[1]

```
#!/bin/sh
# This is a comment!
echo Hello World        # This is a comment, too!
```

Note that to make a file executable, you must set the eXecutable bit, and for a shell script, the Readable bit must also be set:

$ **chmod a+rx first.sh**

$ **./first.sh**

---

1   https://www.shellscript.sh/eg/first.sh.txt

#!/ch/2

2. Philosophy

Shell script programming has a bit of a bad press amongst some Unix systems administrators. This is normally because of one of two things:

- The speed at which an interpreted program will run as compared to a C program, or even an interpreted Perl program.
- Since it is easy to write a simple batch-job type shell script, there are a lot of poor quality shell scripts around.

It is partly due to this that there is a certain machismo associated with creating *good* shell scripts. Scripts which can be used as CGI programs, for example, without losing out too much in speed to Perl (though both would lose to C, in many cases, were speed the only criterion).

There are a number of factors which can go into good, clean, quick, shell scripts.

- The most important criteria must be a clear, readable layout.
- Second is avoiding unnecessary commands.

A clear layout makes the difference between a shell script appearing as "black magic" and one which is easily maintained and understood.

You may be forgiven for thinking that with a simple script, this is not too significant a problem, but two things here are worth bearing in mind.

1. First, a simple script will, more often than anticipated, grow into a large, complex one.
2. Secondly, if nobody else can understand how it works, you will be lumbered with maintaining it yourself for the rest of your life!

Something about shell scripts seems to make them particularly likely to be badly indented, and since the main control structures are if/then/else and loops, indentation is critical for understanding what a script does.

One of the major weaknesses in many shell scripts is lines such as:

```
cat /tmp/myfile | grep "mystring"
```

which would run much faster as:

```
grep "mystring" /tmp/myfile
```

Not much, you may consider; the OS has to load up the /bin/grep executable, which is a reasonably small 75600 bytes on my system, open a pipe in memory for the transfer, load and run the /bin/cat executable, which is an even smaller 9528 bytes on my system, attach it to the input of the pipe, and let it run.

Of course, this kind of thing is what the OS is there for, and it's normally pretty efficient at doing it. But if this command were in a loop being run many times over, the saving of not locating and loading the cat executable, setting up and releasing the pipe, can make some difference, especially in, say, a CGI environment where there are enough other factors to slow things down without the script itself being too much of a hurdle. Some Unices are more efficient than others at what they call "building up and tearing down processes" – i.e., loading them up, executing them, and clearing them away again. But however good your flavour of Unix is at doing this, it'd rather not have to do it at all.

As a result of this, you may hear mention of the Useless Use of Cat Award (UUoC), also known in some circles as **The Award For The Most Gratuitous Use Of The Word Cat In A Serious Shell Script** being bandied about on the `comp.unix.shell` newsgroup from time to time. This is purely a way of peers keeping each other in check, and making sure that things are done right.

Which leads me nicely on to something else: Don't *ever* feel too close to your own shell scripts; by their nature, the source cannot be closed. If you supply a customer with a shell script, s/he can inspect it quite easily. So you might as well accept that it will be inspected by anyone you pass it to; use this to your advantage with the GPL[2] - encourage people to give you feedback and bugfixes for free!

---

2   http://www.gnu.org/copyleft/gpl.html

#!/ch/3

3. A First Script

For our first shell script, we'll just write a script which says "Hello World". We will then try to get more out of a Hello World program than any other tutorial you've ever read :-)
Create a file (`first.sh`) as follows:

first.sh[3]

```
#!/bin/sh
# This is a comment!
echo Hello World    # This is a comment, too!
```

The first line tells Unix that the file is to be executed by `/bin/sh`. This is the standard location of the Bourne shell on just about every Unix system. If you're using GNU/Linux, `/bin/sh` is normally a symbolic link to bash (or, more recently, dash).

The second line begins with a special symbol: #. This marks the line as a comment, and it is ignored completely by the shell. The only exception is when the *very first* line of the file starts with #! - as ours does. This is a special directive which Unix treats specially. It means that even if you are using csh, ksh, or anything else as your interactive shell, that what follows should be interpreted by the Bourne shell.
Similarly, a Perl script may start with the line `#!/usr/bin/perl`

---

3   https://www.shellscript.sh/eg/first.sh.txt

to tell your interactive shell that the program which follows should be executed by Perl. For Bourne shell programming, we shall stick to `#!/bin/sh`.

The third line runs a command: `echo`, with two parameters, or arguments - the first is "`Hello`"; the second is "`World`".
Note that `echo` will automatically put a single space between its parameters.
The `#` symbol still marks a comment; the `#` and anything following it is ignored by the shell.

now run **`chmod 755 first.sh`** to make the text file executable, and run **`./first.sh`**.
Your screen should then look like this:

```
$ chmod 755 first.sh
$ ./first.sh
Hello World
$
```

You will probably have expected that! You could even just run:

```
$ echo Hello World
Hello World
$
```

Now let's make a few changes.
First, note that `echo` puts ONE space between its parameters. Put a few spaces between "Hello" and "World". What do you expect the output to be? What about putting a TAB character between them?
As always with shell programming, try it and see.
The output is exactly the same! We are calling the `echo` program with two arguments; it doesn't care any more than `cp` does about the gaps in between them. Now modify the code again:

```
#!/bin/sh
# This is a comment!
```

Shell Scripting Tutorial

```
echo "Hello    World"    # This is a comment, too!
```

This time it works. You probably expected that, too, if you have experience of other programming languages. But the key to understanding what is going on with more complex command and shell script, is to understand and be able to explain: *Why*? echo has now been called with just one argument - the string "Hello   World". It prints this out exactly.

The point to understand here is that the shell parses the arguments before passing them on to the program being called. In this case, it strips the quotes but passes the string as one argument.

As a final example, type in the following script. Try to predict the outcome before you run it:

first2.sh[4]

```
#!/bin/sh
# This is a comment!
echo "Hello    World"    # This is a comment, too!
echo "Hello World"
echo "Hello * World"
echo Hello * World
echo Hello    World
echo "Hello" World
echo Hello "    " World
echo "Hello \"*\" World"
echo `hello` world
echo 'hello' world
```

Is everything as you expected? If not, don't worry! These are just some of the things we will be covering in this tutorial ... and yes, we will be using more powerful commands than echo!

---

4   https://www.shellscript.sh/eg/first2.sh.txt

Shell Scripting Tutorial

#!/ch/4

4. Variables - Part I

Just about every programming language in existence has the concept of *variables* - a symbolic name for a chunk of memory to which we can assign values, read and manipulate its contents. The Bourne shell is no exception, and this section introduces that idea. This is taken further in Variables - Part II which looks into variables which are set for us by the environment.

Let's look back at our first Hello World example. This could be done using variables (though it's such a simple example that it doesn't really warrant it!)

Note that there must be no spaces around the "=" sign: `VAR=value` works; `VAR = value` doesn't work. In the first case, the shell sees the "=" symbol and treats the command as a variable assignment. In the second case, the shell assumes that `VAR` must be the name of a command and tries to execute it.

If you think about it, this makes sense - how else could you tell it to run the command `VAR` with its first argument being "=" and its second argument being "value"?

Enter the following code into `var1.sh`:

var.sh[5]

```
#!/bin/sh
MY_MESSAGE="Hello World"
echo $MY_MESSAGE
```

---

5   https://www.shellscript.sh/eg/var.sh.txt

This assigns the string "Hello World" to the variable `MY_MESSAGE` then echoes out the value of the variable.

Note that we need the quotes around the string Hello World. Whereas we could get away with `echo Hello World` because `echo` will take any number of parameters, a variable can only hold one value, so a string with spaces must be quoted to that the shell knows to treat it all as one. Otherwise, the shell will try to execute the command `World` after assigning `MY_MESSAGE=Hello`.

The shell does not care about types of variables; they may store strings, integers, real numbers - anything you like.

People used to Perl may be quite happy with this; if you've grown up with C, Pascal, or worse yet Ada, this may seem quite strange. In truth, these are all stored as strings, but routines which expect a number can treat them as such.

If you assign a string to a variable then try to add 1 to it, you will not get away with it:

```
$ x="hello"
$ expr $x + 1
expr: non-numeric argument
$
```

This is because the external program `expr` only expects numbers. But there is no syntactic difference between:

```
MY_MESSAGE="Hello World"
MY_SHORT_MESSAGE=hi
MY_NUMBER=1
MY_PI=3.142
MY_OTHER_PI="3.142"
MY_MIXED=123abc
```

Note though that special characters must be properly escaped to avoid interpretation by the shell.

This is discussed further in Chapter 6, "Escape Characters".

We can interactively set variable names using the `read` command; the following script asks you for your name then greets you personally:

var2.sh

```
#!/bin/sh
echo What is your name?
read MY_NAME
echo "Hello $MY_NAME - hope you're well."
```

Mario Bacinsky kindly pointed out to me that I had originally missed out the double-quotes in line 3, which meant that the single-quote in the word "you're" was unmatched, causing an error. It is this kind of thing which can drive a shell programmer crazy, so watch out for them!

This is using the shell-builtin command `read` which reads a line from standard input into the variable supplied.
Note that even if you give it your full name and don't use double quotes around the `echo` command, it still outputs correctly. How is this done? With the `MY_MESSAGE` variable earlier we had to put double quotes around it to set it.
What happens, is that the `read` command automatically places quotes around its input, so that spaces are treated correctly. (You will need to quote the output, of course - e.g. echo `"$MY_MESSAGE"`).

Scope of Variables

Variables in the Bourne shell do not have to be declared, as they do in languages like C. But if you try to read an undeclared variable, the result is the empty string. You get no warnings or errors. This can cause some subtle bugs - if you assign
`MY_OBFUSCATED_VARIABLE=Hello`
and then

```
echo $MY_OSFUCATED_VARIABLE
```
Then you will get nothing (as the second OBFUSCATED is mis-spelled).

There is a command called export which has a fundamental effect on the scope of variables. In order to really know what's going on with your variables, you will need to understand something about how this is used.

Create a small shell script, myvar2.sh:

---

myvar2.sh[6]

```
#!/bin/sh
echo "MYVAR is: $MYVAR"
MYVAR="hi there"
echo "MYVAR is: $MYVAR"
```

Now run the script:

```
$ ./myvar2.sh
MYVAR is:
MYVAR is: hi there
```

MYVAR hasn't been set to any value, so it's blank. Then we give it a value, and it has the expected result.
Now run:

```
$ MYVAR=hello
$ ./myvar2.sh
MYVAR is:
MYVAR is: hi there
```

It's still not been set! What's going on?!
When you call myvar2.sh from your interactive shell, a new shell

6   https://www.shellscript.sh/eg/myvar2.sh.txt

is spawned to run the script. This is partly because of the
`#!/bin/sh` line at the start of the script, which we discussed
earlier.

We need to `export` the variable for it to be inherited by another
program - including a shell script. Type:

```
$ export MYVAR
$ ./myvar2.sh
MYVAR is: hello
MYVAR is: hi there
```

Now look at line 3 of the script: this is changing the value of
MYVAR. But there is no way that this will be passed back to your
interactive shell. Try reading the value of MYVAR:

```
$ echo $MYVAR
hello
$
```

Once the shell script exits, its environment is destroyed. But MYVAR
keeps its value of hello within your interactive shell.

In order to receive environment changes back from the script, we
must *source* the script - this effectively runs the script within our
own interactive shell, instead of spawning another shell to run it.
We can source a script via the "." (dot) command:

```
$ MYVAR=hello
$ echo $MYVAR
hello
$ . ./myvar2.sh
MYVAR is: hello
MYVAR is: hi there
$ echo $MYVAR
hi there
```

The change has now made it out into our shell again! This is how
your .profile or .bash_profile file works, for example.
Note that in this case, we don't need to export MYVAR.
Thanks to *sway* for pointing out that I'd originally said echo

MYVAR above, not echo $MYVAR as it should be. Another example of an easy mistake to make with shell scripts. One other thing worth mentioning at this point about variables, is to consider the following shell script:

```
#!/bin/sh
echo "What is your name?"
read USER_NAME
echo "Hello $USER_NAME"
echo "I will create you a file called $USER_NAME_file"
touch $USER_NAME_file
```

Think about what result you would expect. For example, if you enter "steve" as your USER_NAME, should the script create steve_file?
Actually, no. This will cause an error unless there is a variable called USER_NAME_file. The shell does not know where the variable ends and the rest starts. How can we define this?
The answer is, that we enclose the variable itself in *curly brackets*:

user.sh[7]

```
#!/bin/sh
echo "What is your name?"
read USER_NAME
echo "Hello $USER_NAME"
echo "I will create you a file called ${USER_NAME}_file"
touch "${USER_NAME}_file"
```

The shell now knows that we are referring to the variable USER_NAME and that we want it suffixed with "_file". This can be

---

7   https://www.shellscript.sh/eg/user.sh.txt

the downfall of many a new shell script programmer, as the source of the problem can be difficult to track down.

Also note the quotes around "`${USER_NAME}_file`" - if the user entered "Steve Parker" (note the space) then without the quotes, the arguments passed to `touch` would be `Steve` and `Parker_file` - that is, we'd effectively be saying `touch Steve Parker_file`, which is two files to be `touch`ed, not one. The quotes avoid this. Thanks to Chris for highlighting this.

#!/ch/5

5. Wildcards

Wildcards are really nothing new if you have used Unix at all before.
It is not necessarily obvious how they are useful in shell scripts though. This section is really just to get the old grey cells thinking how things look when you're in a shell script - predicting what the effect of using different syntaxes are. This will be used later on, particularly in the Loops section.
Think first how you would copy all the files from /tmp/a into /tmp/b. All the .txt files? All the .html files?
Hopefully you will have come up with:

```
$ cp /tmp/a/* /tmp/b/
$ cp /tmp/a/*.txt /tmp/b/
$ cp /tmp/a/*.html /tmp/b/
```

Now how would you list the files in /tmp/a/ without using ls /tmp/a/?
How about echo /tmp/a/*? What are the two key differences between this and the ls output? How can this be useful? Or a hinderance?
How could you rename all .txt files to .bak? Note that

```
$ mv *.txt *.bak
```

will not have the desired effect; think about how this gets expanded by the shell before it is passed to mv. Try this using echo instead of mv if this helps.

We will look into this further later on, as it uses a few concepts not yet covered.

Shell Scripting Tutorial

#!/ch/6

6. Escape Characters

Certain characters are significant to the shell; we have seen, for example, that the use of double quotes (") characters affect how spaces and TAB characters are treated, for example:

```
$ echo Hello        World
Hello World
$ echo "Hello        World"
Hello        World
```

So how do we display: Hello   "World" ?

```
$ echo "Hello    \"World\""
```

The first and last " characters wrap the whole lot into one parameter passed to echo so that the spacing between the two words is kept as is. But the code:

```
$ echo "Hello    " World ""
```

would be interpreted as three parameters:

- "Hello   "
- World
- ""

So the output would be

```
Hello    World
```

Note that we lose the quotes entirely. This is because the first and
second quotes mark off the Hello and following spaces; the
second argument is an unquoted "World" and the third argument
is the empty string; "".

Thanks to Patrick for pointing out that this:

```
$ echo "Hello    "World""
```

is actually only one parameter (no spaces between the quoted
parameters), and that you can test this by replacing the echo
command with (for example) ls.

Most characters (*, ', etc) are not interpreted (i.e., they are taken
literally) by means of placing them in double quotes (""). They are
taken as is and passed on to the command being called. An
example using the asterisk (*) goes:

```
$ echo *
case.shtml escape.shtml first.shtml
functions.shtml hints.shtml index.shtml
ip-primer.txt raid1+0.txt
$ echo *txt
ip-primer.txt raid1+0.txt
$ echo "*"
*
$ echo "*txt"
*txt
```

In the first example, * is expanded to mean all files in the current
directory. In the second example, *txt means all files ending in
txt. In the third, we put the * in double quotes, and it is
interpreted literally. In the fourth example, the same applies, but
we have appended txt to the string.

However, ", $, `, and \ are still interpreted by the shell, even when they're in double quotes. The backslash (\) character is used to mark these special characters so that they are not interpreted by the shell, but passed on to the command being run (for example, echo). So to output the string: (Assuming that the value of $X is 5):

```
A quote is ", backslash is \, backtick is `.
A few spaces are    and dollar is $. $X is 5.
```

we would have to write:

```
$ echo "A quote is \", backslash is \\, backtick is \`."
A quote is ", backslash is \, backtick is `.
$ echo "A few spaces are    ; dollar is \$. \$X is ${X}."
A few spaces are    ; dollar is $. $X is 5.
```

We have seen why the " is special for preserving spacing. Dollar ($) is special because it marks a variable, so $X is replaced by the shell with the contents of the variable X. Backslash (\) is special because it is itself used to mark other characters off; we need the following options for a complete shell:

```
$ echo "This is \\ a backslash"
This is \ a backslash
$ echo "This is \" a quote and this is \\ a backslash"
This is " a quote and this is \ a backslash
```

So backslash itself must be escaped to show that it is to be taken literally. The other special character, the backtick, is discussed later in Chapter 12, "External Programs."

#!/ch/7

7. Loops

Most languages have the concept of loops: If we want to repeat a task twenty times, we don't want to have to type in the code twenty times, with maybe a slight change each time. As a result, we have `for` and `while` loops in the Bourne shell. This is somewhat fewer features than other languages, but nobody claimed that shell programming has the power of C.

For Loops

`for` loops iterate through a set of values until the list is exhausted:

for.sh[8]

```
#!/bin/sh
for i in 1 2 3 4 5
do
  echo "Looping ... number $i"
done
```

Try this code and see what it does. Note that the values can be anything at all:

---

8   https://www.shellscript.sh/eg/for.sh.txt

for2.sh[9]

```
#!/bin/sh
for i in hello 1 * 2 goodbye
do
  echo "Looping ... i is set to $i"
done
```

This is well worth trying. Make sure that you understand what is happening here. Try it without the * and grasp the idea, then re-read the Wildcards section and try it again with the * in place. Try it also in different directories, and with the * surrounded by double quotes, and try it preceded by a backslash (*)

In case you don't have access to a shell at the moment (it is very useful to have a shell to hand whilst reading this tutorial), the results of the above two scripts are:

```
Looping .... number 1
Looping .... number 2
Looping .... number 3
Looping .... number 4
Looping .... number 5
```

and, for the second example:

```
Looping ... i is set to hello
Looping ... i is set to 1
Looping ... i is set to (name of first file in current
directory)
       ... etc ...
Looping ... i is set to (name of last file in current
directory)
Looping ... i is set to 2
Looping ... i is set to goodbye
```

So, as you can see, for simply loops through whatever input it is

---

9   https://www.shellscript.sh/eg/for2.sh.txt

given, until it runs out of input.

While Loops

while loops can be much more fun! (depending on your idea of fun, and how often you get out of the house...)

while.sh[10]

```
#!/bin/sh
INPUT_STRING=hello
while [ "$INPUT_STRING" != "bye" ]
do
   echo "Please type something in (bye to quit)"
   read INPUT_STRING
   echo "You typed: $INPUT_STRING"
done
```

What happens here, is that the echo and read statements will run indefinitely until you type "**bye**" when prompted. Review "Variables - Part I" (Chapter 4) to see why we set INPUT_STRING=hello before testing it. This makes it a repeat loop, not a traditional while loop.

The colon (:) always evaluates to true; whilst using this can be necessary sometimes, it is often preferable to use a real exit condition. Compare quitting the above loop with the one below; see which is the more elegant. Also think of some situations in which each one would be more useful than the other:

---

10   https://www.shellscript.sh/eg/while.sh.txt

while2.sh[11]

```sh
#!/bin/sh
while :
do
  echo "Please type something in (^C to quit)"
  read INPUT_STRING
  echo "You typed: $INPUT_STRING"
done
```

Another useful trick is the while read f loop. This example uses the case statement, which we'll cover later. It reads from the file myfile, and for each line, tells you what language it thinks is being used. Each line must end with a LF (newline) - if cat myfile doesn't end with a blank line, that final line will not be processed.

while3a.sh[12]

```sh
#!/bin/sh
while read f
do
  case $f in
        hello)          echo English    ;;
        howdy)          echo American    ;;
        gday)           echo Australian  ;;
        bonjour)        echo French      ;;
        "guten tag")    echo German      ;;
        *)              echo Unknown Language: $f
                ;;
  esac
done < myfile
```

11 https://www.shellscript.sh/eg/while2.sh.txt
12 https://www.shellscript.sh/eg/while3a.sh.txt

Shell Scripting Tutorial

On many Unix systems, this can also be done as:

while3b.sh[13]

```
#!/bin/sh
while f=`line`
do
   .. process f ..
done < myfile
```

But since the while read f works with any *nix, and doesn't depend on the external program line, the former is preferable. See "External Programs" (Chapter 12) to see why this method uses the backtick (`). Had I referred to $i (not $f) in the default ("Unknown Language") case above, there would have been no warnings or errors, even though $i has not been declared or defined. For example:

```
$ i=THIS_IS_A_BUG
$ export i
$ ./while3.sh something
Unknown Language: THIS_IS_A_BUG
$
```

So make sure that you avoid typos. This is also another good reason for using ${x} and not just $x - if x="A" and you want to say "A1", you need echo ${x}1, as echo $x1 will try to use the variable x1, which may not exist, or may be set to "B2," or anything else unexpected.

I recently found an old thread on Usenet which I had been

---

13   https://www.shellscript.sh/eg/while3b.sh.txt

involved in, where I actually learned more ... Google has it here.
14

A handy Bash (but not Bourne Shell) tip I learned from the Linux
From Scratch[15] project is:

```
mkdir rc{0,1,2,3,4,5,6,S}.d
```

instead of the more cumbersome:

```
for runlevel in 0 1 2 3 4 5 6 S
do
  mkdir rc${runlevel}.d
done
```

And this can be done recursively, too:

```
$ cd /
$ ls -ld {,usr,usr/local}/{bin,sbin,lib}
drwxr-xr-x   2 root     root      4096 Oct 26 01:00 /bin
drwxr-xr-x   6 root     root      4096 Jan 16 17:09 /lib
drwxr-xr-x   2 root     root      4096 Oct 27 00:02 /sbin
drwxr-xr-x   2 root     root     40960 Jan 16 19:35 usr/bin
drwxr-xr-x  83 root     root     49152 Jan 16 17:23 usr/lib
drwxr-xr-x   2 root     root      4096 Jan 16 22:22 usr/local/bin
drwxr-xr-x   3 root     root      4096 Jan 16 19:17 usr/local/lib
drwxr-xr-x   2 root     root      4096 Dec 28 00:44 usr/local/sbin
drwxr-xr-x   2 root     root      8192 Dec 27 02:10 usr/sbin
```

We will use while loops further in the Test and Case chapters.

---

14 https://groups.google.com/forum/?hl=en#!
    msg/comp.unix.shell/Tp5JElzydBo/n7f8gmrn1S0J
15 http://www.linuxfromscratch.org/

Shell Scripting Tutorial

#!/ch/8

8. Test

test is used by virtually every shell script written. It may not seem that way, because test is not often called directly. test is more frequently called as [. [is a symbolic link to test, just to make shell programs more readable. If is also normally a shell builtin (which means that the shell itself will interpret [as meaning test, even if your Unix environment is set up differently):

```
$ type [
[ is a shell builtin
$ which [
/usr/bin/[
$ ls -l /usr/bin/[
lrwxrwxrwx 1 root root 4 Mar 27 2000 /usr/bin/[ -> test
```

This means that '[' is actually a program, just like ls and other programs, so it must be surrounded by spaces:

```
if [$foo = "bar" ]
```

will not work; it is interpreted as if test$foo = "bar"], which is a ']' without a beginning '['. Put spaces around all your operators. I've highlighted the mandatory spaces with the word 'SPACE' - replace 'SPACE' with an actual space; if there isn't a space there, it won't work:

```
if SPACE [ SPACE "$foo" SPACE = SPACE "bar" SPACE ]
```

Note: Some shells also accept "==" for string comparison; this is not portable, a single "=" should be used for strings, or "-eq" for integers.

test is a simple but powerful comparison utility. For full details, run man test on your system, but here are some usages and typical examples.

test is most often invoked indirectly via the if and while statements. It is also the reason you will come into difficulties if you create a program called test and try to run it, as this shell builtin will be called instead of your program! The syntax for if...then...else... is:

```
if [ ... ]
then
  # if-code
else
  # else-code
fi
```

Note that fi is if backwards! This is used again later with case and esac. Also, be aware of the syntax - the "if [...]" and the "then" commands must be on different lines. Alternatively, the semicolon ";" can separate them:

```
if [ ... ]; then
  # do something
fi
```

You can also use the elif, like this:

```
if  [ something ]; then
 echo "Something"
 elif [ something_else ]; then
   echo "Something else"
 else
   echo "None of the above"
fi
```

Shell Scripting Tutorial

This will echo "Something" if the [something] test succeeds, otherwise it will test [something_else], and echo "Something else" if that succeeds. If all else fails, it will echo "None of the above".

Try the following code snippet, before running it set the variable X to various values (try -1, 0, 1, hello, bye, etc). You can do this as follows (thanks to Dave for pointing out the need to export the variable, as noted in Variables - Part I.):

```
$ X=5
$ export X
$ ./test.sh
   ... output of test.sh ...
$ X=hello
$ ./test.sh
   ... output of test.sh ...
$ X=test.sh
$ ./test.sh
   ... output of test.sh ...
```

Then try it again, with $X as the name of an existing file, such as /etc/hosts.

---

test.sh[16]

```
#!/bin/sh
if [ "$X" -lt "0" ]
then
  echo "X is less than zero"
fi
if [ "$X" -gt "0" ]; then
  echo "X is more than zero"
fi
[ "$X" -le "0" ] && \
    echo "X is less than or equal to  zero"
[ "$X" -ge "0" ] && \
    echo "X is more than or equal to zero"
```

---

16 https://www.shellscript.sh/eg/test.sh.txt

```
[ "$X" = "0" ] && \
    echo "X is the string or number \"0\""
[ "$X" = "hello" ] && \
    echo "X matches the string \"hello\""
[ "$X" != "hello" ] && \
    echo "X is not the string \"hello\""
[ -n "$X" ] && \
    echo "X is of nonzero length"
[ -f "$X" ] && \
    echo "X is the path of a real file" || \
    echo "No such file: $X"
[ -x "$X" ] && \
    echo "X is the path of an executable file"
[ "$X" -nt "/etc/passwd" ] && \
    echo "X is a file which is newer than /etc/passwd"
```

Note that we can use the semicolon (;) to join two lines together. This is often done to save a bit of space in simple if statements. The backslash simply tells the shell that this is not the end of the line, but the two (or more) lines should be treated as one. This is useful for readability. It is customary to indent the following line.

As we see from these examples, test can perform many tests on numbers, strings, and filenames.

Thanks to Aaron for pointing out that -a, -e (both meaning "file exists"), -S (file is a Socket), -nt (file is newer than), -ot (file is older than), -ef (paths refer to the same file) and -O (file is owned my user), are not available in the traditional Bourne shell (eg, /bin/sh on Solaris, AIX, HPUX, etc).

There is a simpler way of writing if statements: The && and || commands give code to run if the result is true.

```
#!/bin/sh
[ $X -ne 0 ] && echo "X isn't zero" || echo "X is zero"
[ -f $X ] && echo "X is a file" || echo "X is not a file"
[ -n $X ] && echo "X is of non-zero length" || \
    echo "X is of zero length"
```

Shell Scripting Tutorial

This syntax is possible because there is a file (or shell-builtin) called [which is linked to test. Be careful using this construct, though, as overuse can lead to very hard-to-read code. The if...then...else... structure is much more readable. Use of the [...] construct is recommended for while loops and trivial sanity checks with which you do not want to overly distract the reader.

Note that when you set X to a non-numeric value, the first few comparisons result in the message:

```
test.sh: [: integer expression expected before -lt
test.sh: [: integer expression expected before -gt
test.sh: [: integer expression expected before -le
test.sh: [: integer expression expected before -ge
```

This is because the -lt, -gt, -le and -ge comparisons are only designed for integers, and do not work on strings. The string comparisons, such as != will happily treat "5" as a string, but there is no sensible way of treating "Hello" as an integer, so the integer comparisons complain. If you want your shell script to behave more gracefully, you will have to check the contents of the variable before you test it - maybe something like this:

```
echo -en "Please guess the magic number: "
read X
echo $X | grep "[^0-9]" > /dev/null 2>&1
if [ "$?" -eq "0" ]; then
  # If the grep found something other than 0-9
  # then it's not an integer.
  echo "Sorry, wanted a number"
else
  # The grep found only 0-9, so it's an integer.
  # We can safely do a test on it.
  if [ "$X" = "7" ]; then
    echo "You entered the magic number!"
  fi
fi
```

In this way you can echo a more meaningful message to the user, and exit gracefully. The $? variable is explained in "Variables -

Part II" (Chapter 10), and grep is a complicated beast, so here goes: grep [0-9] finds lines of text which contain digits (0-9) and possibly other characters, so the caret (^) in grep [^0-9] finds only those lines which don't consist only of numbers. We can then take the opposite (by acting on failure, not success). Okay? The >/dev/null 2>&1 directs any output or errors to the special "null" device, instead of going to the user's screen. Many thanks to Paul Schermerhorn for correcting me - this page used to claim that grep -v [0-9] would work, but this is clearly far too simplistic.

We can use test in while loops as follows:

test2.sh[17]

```
#!/bin/sh
X=0
while [ -n "$X" ]
do
   echo "Enter some text (RETURN to quit)"
   read X
   echo "You said: $X"
done
```

This code will keep asking for input until you hit RETURN (X is zero length). Thanks to Justin Heath for pointing out that the script didn't work - I'd missed out the quotes around $X in the while [-n "$X"]. Without those quotes, there is nothing to test when $X is empty. Alexander Weber has pointed out that running this script will end untidily:

```
$ ./test2.sh
Enter some text (RETURN to quit)
```

17 https://www.shellscript.sh/eg/test2.sh.txt

```
fred
You said: fred
Enter some text (RETURN to quit)
wilma
You said: wilma
Enter some text (RETURN to quit)

You said:
$
```

This can be tidied up with another test within the loop:

#!/bin/sh

```
X=0
while [ -n "$X" ]
do
  echo "Enter some text (RETURN to quit)"
  read X
  if [ -n "$X" ]; then
    echo "You said: $X"
  fi
done
```

Note also that I've used two different syntaxes for if statements on this page. These are:

```
if [ "$X" -lt "0" ]
then
  echo "X is less than zero"
fi
```

.... and ....

```
if [ ! -n "$X" ]; then
  echo "You said: $X"
fi
```

You must have a break between the if statement and the then construct. This can be a semicolon or a newline, it doesn't matter which, but there must be one or the other between the if and the then. It would be nice to just say:

```
if [ ! -n "$X" ]
  echo "You said: $X"
```

but the then and fi are absolutely required.

9. Case

The `case` statement saves going through a whole set of `if` ..
then .. `else` statements. Its syntax is really quite simple:

talk.sh[18]

```
#!/bin/sh

echo "Please talk to me ..."
while :
do
  read INPUT_STRING
  case $INPUT_STRING in
        hello)
                echo "Hello yourself!"
                ;;
        bye)
                echo "See you again!"
                break
                ;;
        *)
                echo "Sorry, I don't understand"
                ;;
  esac
done
echo
echo "That's all folks!"
```

18 https://www.shellscript.sh/eg/talk.sh.txt

Okay, so it's not the best conversationalist in the world; it's only an example!

Try running it and check how it works...

```
$ ./talk.sh
Please talk to me ...
hello
Hello yourself!
What do you think of politics?
Sorry, I don't understand
bye
See you again!

That's all folks!
$
```

The syntax is quite simple: The case line itself is always of the same format, and it means that we are testing the value of the variable INPUT_STRING.

The options we understand are then listed and followed by a right bracket, as hello) and bye). This means that if INPUT_STRING matches hello then that section of code is executed, up to the double semicolon. If INPUT_STRING matches "bye" then the "goodbye" message is printed and the loop exits. Note that if we wanted to exit the script completely then we would use the command exit instead of break. The third option here, the *), is the default catch-all condition; it is not required, but is often useful for debugging purposes even if we think we know what values the test variable will have.

The whole case statement is ended with esac (case backwards!) then we end the while loop with a done.

That's about as complicated as case conditions get, but they can be a very useful and powerful tool. They are often used to parse the parameters passed to a shell script, amongst other uses.

Shell Scripting Tutorial

#!/ch/10

10. Variables - Part II

There are a set of variables which are set for you already, and
most of these cannot have values assigned to them. These can
contain useful information, which can be used by the script to
know about the environment in which it is running.

The first set of variables we will look at are $0 .. $9 and $#. The
variable $0 is the *basename* of the program as it was called. $1 ..
$9 are the first 9 additional parameters the script was called with.
The variable $@ is all parameters $1 .. whatever. The variable
$*, is similar, but does not preserve any whitespace, and quoting,
so "File with spaces" becomes "File" "with" "spaces". This is similar
to the echo stuff we looked at in A First Script. As a general rule,
use $@ and avoid $*. $# is the number of parameters the script
was called with. Let's take an example script:

var3.sh[19]

```
#!/bin/sh
echo "I was called with $# parameters"
echo "My name is $0"
echo "My first parameter is $1"
echo "My second parameter is $2"
echo "All parameters are $@"
```

---

19 https://www.shellscript.sh/eg/var3.sh.txt

Let's look at running this code and see the output:

```
$ /home/steve/var3.sh
I was called with 0 parameters
My name is /home/steve/var3.sh
My first parameter is
My second parameter is
All parameters are
$
$ ./var3.sh hello world earth
I was called with 3 parameters
My name is ./var3.sh
My first parameter is hello
My second parameter is world
All parameters are hello world earth
```

Note that the value of $0 changes depending on how the script was called. The external utility basename can help tidy this up:

```
echo "My name is `basename $0`"
```

$# and $1 .. $2 are set automatically by the shell. We can take more than 9 parameters by using the shift command; look at the script below:

var4.sh[20]

```
#!/bin/sh
while [ "$#" -gt "0" ]
do
   echo "\$1 is $1"
   shift
done
```

This script keeps on using shift until $# is down to zero, at which point the list is empty.

---

20 https://www.shellscript.sh/eg/var4.sh.txt

Another special variable is $?. This contains the exit value of the last run command. So the code:

```
#!/bin/sh
/usr/local/bin/my-command
if [ "$?" -ne "0" ]; then
  echo "Sorry, we had a problem there!"
fi
```

will attempt to run /usr/local/bin/my-command which should exit with a value of zero if all went well, or a nonzero value on failure. We can then handle this by checking the value of $? after calling the command. This helps make scripts robust and more intelligent. Well-behaved applications should return zero on success. Hence the quote:

> "One of the main causes of the fall of the Roman Empire
> was that, lacking zero, they had no way to indicate
> successful termination of their C Programs." (Robert Firth)

The other two main variables set for you by the environment are $$ and $!. These are both process numbers. The $$ variable is the PID (Process IDentifier) of the currently running shell. This can be useful for creating temporary files, such as /tmp/my-script.$$ which is useful if many instances of the script could be run at the same time, and they all need their own temporary files. The $! variable is the PID of the last run background process. This is useful to keep track of the process as it gets on with its job.

Another interesting variable is IFS. This is the *Internal Field Separator*. The default value is SPACE TAB NEWLINE, but if you are changing it, it's easier to take a copy, as shown:

var5.sh[21]

```sh
#!/bin/sh
old_IFS="$IFS"
IFS=:
echo "Please input some data separated by colons ..."
read x y z
IFS=$old_IFS
echo "x is $x y is $y z is $z"
```

This script runs like this:

```
$ ./ifs.sh
Please input some data separated by colons ...
hello:how are you:today
x is hello y is how are you z is today
```

Note that if you enter: "hello:how are you:today:my:friend" then the output would be:

```
$ ./ifs.sh
Please input some data separated by colons ...
hello:how are you:today:my:friend
x is hello y is how are you z is today:my:friend
```

It is important when dealing with IFS in particular (but any variable not entirely under your control) to realise that it could contain spaces, newlines and other "uncontrollable" characters. It is therefore a very good idea to use double-quotes around it, ie: old_IFS="$IFS" instead of old_IFS=$IFS.

---

21 https://www.shellscript.sh/eg/var5.sh.txt

Shell Scripting Tutorial

#!/ch/11

11. Variables - Part III

As we mentioned in Chapter 4 ("Variables - Part I"), curly brackets around a variable avoid confusion:

```
foo=sun
echo $fooshine      # $fooshine is undefined
echo ${foo}shine    # displays the word "sunshine"
```

That's not all, though - these fancy brackets have a another, much more powerful use. We can deal with issues of variables being undefined or null (in the shell, there's not much difference between undefined and null).

Using Default Values

Consider the following code snippet which prompts the user for input, but accepts defaults:

```
#!/bin/sh
echo -en "What is your name [ `whoami` ] "
read myname
if [ -z "$myname" ]; then
  myname=`whoami`
fi
echo "Your name is : $myname"
```

Passing the "-en" to echo tells it not to add a linebreak (for bash and csh). For Dash, Bourne and other compliant shells, you use a "\c" at the end of the line, instead. Ksh understands both forms.

This script runs like this if you accept the default by pressing "RETURN":

```
steve$ ./name.sh
What is your name [ steve ] RETURN
Your name is : steve
```

... or, with user input:

```
steve$ ./name.sh
What is your name [ steve ] foo
Your name is : foo
```

This could be done better using a shell variable feature. By using curly braces and the special ":-" usage, you can specify a default value to use if the variable is unset:

```
echo -en "What is your name [ `whoami` ] "
read myname
echo "Your name is : ${myname:-`whoami`}"
```

This could be considered a special case – we're using the output of the whoami command, which prints your login namc (UID). The more canonical example is to use fixed text, like this:

```
echo "Your name is : ${myname:-John Doe}"
```

As with other use of the backticks, `whoami` runs in a subshell, so any cd commands, or setting any other variables, within the backticks, will not affect the currently-running shell.

Using and Setting Default Values

There is another syntax, ":=", which sets the variable to the default if it is undefined:

```
echo "Your name is : ${myname:=John Doe}"
```

This technique means that any subsequent access to the $myname variable will always get a value, either entered by the user, or "John Doe" otherwise.

#!/ch/12

12. External Programs

External programs are often used within shell scripts; there are a few builtin commands (echo, which, and test are commonly builtin), but many useful commands are actually Unix utilities, such as tr, grep, expr and cut.

The backtick (`)is also often associated with external commands. Because of this, we will discuss the backtick first. The backtick is used to indicate that the enclosed text is to be executed as a command. This is quite simple to understand. First, use an interactive shell to read your full name from /etc/passwd:

```
$ grep "^${USER}:" /etc/passwd | cut -d: -f5
Steve Parker
```

Now we will grab this output into a variable which we can manipulate more easily:

```
$ MYNAME=`grep "^${USER}:" /etc/passwd | cut -d: -f5`
$ echo $MYNAME
Steve Parker
```

So we see that the backtick simply catches the standard output from any command or set of commands we choose to run. It can also improve performance if you want to run a slow command or set of commands and parse various bits of its output:

```
#!/bin/sh
find / -name "*.html" -print | grep "/index.html$"
find / -name "*.html" -print | grep "/contents.html$"
```

This code could take a long time to run, and we are doing it twice! A better solution is:

```
#!/bin/sh
HTML_FILES=`find / -name "*.html" -print`
echo "$HTML_FILES" | grep "/index.html$"
echo "$HTML_FILES" | grep "/contents.html$"
```

Note: the quotes around $HTML_FILES are essential to preserve the newlines between each file listed. Otherwise, grep will see one huge long line of text, and not one line per file.

This way, we are only running the slow find once, roughly halving the execution time of the script.

We discuss specific examples further in Chapter 14, the Hints and Tips section of this tutorial.

#!/ch/13

13. Functions

One often-overlooked feature of Bourne shell script programming
is that you can easily write functions for use within your script.
This is generally done in one of two ways; with a simple script,
the function is simply declared in the same file as it is called.
However, when writing a suite of scripts, it is often easier to write
a "library" of useful functions, and source that file at the start of
the other scripts which use the functions. This will be shown
later. The method is the same however it is done; we will
primarily be using the first way here. The second (library)
method is basically the same, except that the command

```
. ./library.sh
```

goes at the start of the script.

There could be some confusion about whether to call shell
functions *procedures* or *functions*; the definition of a function is
traditionally that is returns a single value, and does not output
anything. A procedure, on the other hand, does not return a
value, but may produce output. A shell function may do neither,
either or both. It is generally accepted that in shell scripts they are
called functions.

A function may return a value in one of four different ways:

- Change the state of a variable or variables
- Use the exit command to end the shell script

- Use the `return` command to end the function, and return the supplied value to the calling section of the shell script
- echo output to stdout, which will be caught by the caller just as c=`expr $a + $b` is caught

This is rather like C, in that `exit` stops the program, and `return` returns control to the caller. The difference is that a shell function cannot change its parameters, though it can change global parameters.

A simple script using a function would look like this:

function.sh[22]

```
#!/bin/sh
# A simple script with a function...

add_a_user()
{
  USER=$1
  PASSWORD=$2
  shift; shift;
  # Having shifted twice, the rest is now comments ...
  COMMENTS=$@
  echo "Adding user $USER ..."
  echo useradd -c "$COMMENTS" $USER
  echo passwd $USER $PASSWORD
  echo "Added user $USER ($COMMENTS) with pass $PASSWORD"
}

###
# Main body of script starts here
###
echo "Start of script..."
add_a_user bob letmein Bob Holness the presenter
add_a_user fred badpassword Fred Durst the singer
add_a_user bilko worsepassword Sgt. Bilko the role model
echo "End of script..."
```

---

22 https://www.shellscript.sh/eg/function.sh.txt

Line 4 identifies itself as a function declaration by ending in (). This is followed by {, and everything following to the matching } is taken to be the code of that function. This code is *not executed* until the function is called. Functions are read in, but basically ignored until they are actually called.

Note that for this example the `useradd` and `passwd` commands have been prefixed with `echo` - this is a useful debugging technique to check that the right commands would be executed. It also means that you can run the script without being root or adding dodgy user accounts to your system!

We have been used to the idea that a shell script is executed sequentially. This is not so with functions. In this case, the function `add_a_user` is read in and checked for syntax, but not executed until it is explicitly called. Execution starts with the `echo` statement "Start of script...". The next line, `add_a_user bob letmein Bob Holness` is recognised as a function call so the `add_a_user` function is entered and starts executing with certain additions to the environment:

```
$1=bob
$2=letmein
$3=Bob
$4=Holness
$5=the
$6=presenter
```

So within that function, $1 is set to `bob`, regardless of what $1 may be set to outside of the function. So if we want to refer to the "original" $1 *inside* the function, we have to assign a name to it - such as: A=$1 before we call the function. Then, within the function, we can refer to $A. We use the `shift` command again to get the $3 and onwards parameters into $@. The function then adds the user and sets their password. It `echoes` a comment to that effect, and returns control to the next line of the main code.

Scope of Variables

Programmers used to other languages may be surprised at the scope rules for shell functions. Basically, there is no scoping, other than the parameters ($1, $2, $@, etc). Taking the following simple code segment:

```
#!/bin/sh

myfunc()
{
  echo "I was called as : $@"
  x=2
}

### Main script starts here

echo "Script was called with $@"
x=1
echo "x is $x"
myfunc 1 2 3
echo "x is $x"
```

The script, when called as scope.sh a b c, gives the following output:

```
Script was called with a b c
x is 1
I was called as : 1 2 3
x is 2
```

The $@ parameters are changed within the function to reflect how the function was called. The variable x, however, is effectively a global variable - myfunc changed it, and that change is still effective when control returns to the main script.

A function will be called in a sub-shell if its output is piped somewhere else - that is, "myfunc 1 2 3 | tee out.log" will still say "x is 1" the second time around. This is because a new shell process is called to pipe myfunc(). This can make debugging very frustrating; Astrid had a script which suddenly failed when the "| tee" was added, and it is not immediately obvious why this must be. The tee has to be started up before the function to the left of the pipe; with the simple example of "ls | grep foo", then grep has to be started first, with its stdin then tied to the stdout of ls once ls starts. In the shell script, the shell has already been started before we even knew we were going to pipe through tee, so the operating system has to start tee, then start a new shell to call myfunc(). This is frustrating, but well worth being aware of.

Functions cannot change the values they have been called with, either - this must be done by changing the variables themselves, not the parameters as passed to the script. An example shows this more clearly:

```
#!/bin/sh

myfunc()
{
  echo "\$1 is $1"
  echo "\$2 is $2"
  # cannot change $1 - we'd have to say:
  # 1="Goodbye Cruel"
  # which is not a valid syntax. However, we can
  # change $a:
  a="Goodbye Cruel"
}

### Main script starts here

a=Hello
b=World
myfunc $a $b
echo "a is $a"
echo "b is $b"
```

This rather cynical function changes $a, so the message "Hello World" becomes "Goodbye Cruel World".

Recursion

Functions can be recursive - here's a simple example of a factorial function:

---

factorial.sh[23]

```
#!/bin/sh

factorial()
{
  if [ "$1" -gt "1" ]; then
    i=`expr $1 - 1`
    j=`factorial $i`
    k=`expr $1 \* $j`
    echo $k
  else
    echo 1
  fi
}

while :
do
  echo "Enter a number:"
  read x
  factorial $x
done
```

As promised, we will now briefly discuss using libraries between shell scripts. These can also be used to define common variables, as we shall see.

---

23 https://www.shellscript.sh/eg/factorial.sh.txt

common.lib[24]

```
# common.lib
# Note no #!/bin/sh as this should not spawn
# an extra shell. It's not the end of the world
# to have one, but clearer not to.
#
STD_MSG="About to rename some files..."

rename()
{
  # expects to be called as: rename .txt .bak
  FROM=$1
  TO=$2

  for i in *$FROM
  do
    j=`basename $i $FROM`
    mv $i ${j}$TO
  done
}
```

function2.sh[25]

```
#!/bin/sh
# function2.sh
. ./common.lib
echo $STD_MSG
rename txt bak
```

function3.sh[26]

```
#!/bin/sh
# function3.sh
. ./common.lib
echo $STD_MSG
rename html html-bak
```

---

24 https://www.shellscript.sh/eg/common.lib.txt
25 https://www.shellscript.sh/eg/function2.sh.txt
26 https://www.shellscript.sh/eg/function3.sh.txt

Here we see two user shell scripts, `function2.sh` and `function3.sh`, each *source*ing the common library file `common.lib`, and using variables and functions declared in that file. This is nothing too earth-shattering, just an example of how code reuse can be done in shell programming.

Exit Codes

For details about exit codes, see the *Exit Codes* part of the Hints and Tips section (Chapter 14) of the tutorial. For now, though we shall briefly look at the `return` call.

```
#!/bin/sh

adduser()
{
  USER=$1
  PASSWD=$2
  shift ; shift
  COMMENTS=$@
  useradd -c "${COMMENTS}" $USER
  if [ "$?" -ne "0" ]; then
    echo "Useradd failed"
    return 1
  fi
  passwd $USER $PASSWD
  if [ "$?" -ne "0" ]; then
    echo "Setting password failed"
    return 2
  fi
  echo "Added user $USER ($COMMENTS) with pass $PASSWORD"
}

## Main script starts here

adduser bob letmein Bob Holness from Blockbusters
if [ "$?" -eq "1" ]; then
```

```
    echo "Something went wrong with useradd"
elif [ "$?" -eq "2" ]; then
    echo "Something went wrong with passwd"
else
    echo "Bob Holness added to the system."
fi
```

This script checks the two external calls it makes (useradd and passwd), and lets the user know if they fail. The function then defines a return code of 1 to indicate any problem with useradd, and 2 to indicate any problem with passwd. That way, the calling script knows where the problem lay.

#!/ch/14

14. Hints and Tips

Unix is full of text manipulating utilities, some of the more powerful of which we will now discuss in this section of this tutorial. The significance of this, is that virtually everything under Unix *is* text. Virtually anything you can think of is controlled by either a text file, or by a command-line-interface (CLI). The only thing you can't automate using a shell script is a GUI-only utility or feature. And under Unix, there aren't too many of them!

You may have heard it said, that, with *nix, "everything is a file" - it's true.

We have a few subsections here ... what follows is general advice, hints and tips.

CGI Scripting

For CGI programming, there are a couple of extra variables to be aware of, and a few tips I've picked up along the way. Although the shell may not seem the obvious choice for CGI programming, it is quick to write and simple to debug. As such, it makes for an ideal prototyping language for CGI scripts, and fine for simple or little-used CGI scripts permanently. cookie.cgi - which calls fortune.cgi

Exit Codes

Exit codes are a number between 0 and 255, which is returned by any Unix command when it returns control to its parent process. Other numbers can be used, but these are treated modulo 256, so `exit -10` is equivalent to `exit 246`, and `exit 257` is equivalent to `exit 1`.

These can be used within a shell script to change the flow of execution depending on the success or failure of commands executed. This was briefly introduced in Chapter 10, "Variables - Part II". Here we shall look in more detail in the available interpretations of exit codes.

Success is traditionally represented with `exit 0`; *failure* is normally indicated with a non-zero exit-code. This value can indicate different reasons for failure. For example, GNU `grep` returns 0 on success, 1 if no matches were found, and 2 for other errors (syntax errors, non-existent input files, etc).

We shall look at three different methods for checking error status, and discuss the pros and cons of each approach.

Firstly, the simple approach:

```
#!/bin/sh
# First attempt at checking return codes
USERNAME=`grep "^${1}:" /etc/passwd|cut -d":" -f1`
if [ "$?" -ne "0" ]; then
  echo "Sorry, cannot find user ${1} in /etc/passwd"
  exit 1
fi
NAME=`grep "^${1}:" /etc/passwd|cut -d":" -f5`
HOMEDIR=`grep "^${1}:" /etc/passwd|cut -d":" -f6`

echo "USERNAME: $USERNAME"
echo "NAME: $NAME"
echo "HOMEDIR: $HOMEDIR"
```

Shell Scripting Tutorial

This script works fine if you supply a valid username in /etc/passwd. However, if you enter an invalid code, it does not do what you might at first expect - it keeps running, and just shows:

```
USERNAME:
NAME:
HOMEDIR:
```

Why is this? As mentioned, the $? variable is set to the return code of the *last executed command*. In this case, that is cut. cut had no problems which it feels like reporting - as far as I can tell from testing it, and reading the documentation, cut returns zero whatever happens! It was fed an empty string, and did its job - returned the first field of its input, which just happened to be the empty string. So what do we do? If we have an error here, grep will report it, not cut. Therefore, we have to test grep's return code, not cut's.

```
#!/bin/sh
# Second attempt at checking return codes
grep "^${1}:" /etc/passwd > /dev/null 2>&1
if [ "$?" -ne "0" ]; then
  echo "Sorry, cannot find user ${1} in /etc/passwd"
  exit 1
fi
USERNAME=`grep "^${1}:" /etc/passwd|cut -d":" -f1`
NAME=`grep "^${1}:" /etc/passwd|cut -d":" -f5`
HOMEDIR=`grep "^${1}:" /etc/passwd|cut -d":" -f6`

echo "USERNAME: $USERNAME"
echo "NAME: $NAME"
echo "HOMEDIR: $HOMEDIR"
```

This fixes the problem for us, though at the expense of slightly longer code. That is the basic way which textbooks might show you, but it is far from being all there is to know about error-checking in shell scripts. This method may not be the most suitable to your particular command-sequence, or may be unmaintainable. Below, we shall investigate two alternative approaches.

As a second approach, we can tidy this somewhat by putting the test into a separate function, instead of littering the code with lots of 4-line tests:

```
#!/bin/sh
# A Tidier approach

check_errs()
{
  # Function. Parameter 1 is the return code
  # Para. 2 is text to display on failure.
  if [ "${1}" -ne "0" ]; then
    echo "ERROR # ${1} : ${2}"
    # as a bonus, make our script exit with the right
error code.
    exit ${1}
  fi
}

### main script starts here ###

grep "^${1}:" /etc/passwd > /dev/null 2>&1
check_errs $? "User ${1} not found in /etc/passwd"
USERNAME=`grep "^${1}:" /etc/passwd|cut -d":" -f1`
check_errs $? "Cut returned an error"
echo "USERNAME: $USERNAME"
check_errs $? "echo returned an error - very strange!"
```

This allows us to test for errors 3 times, with customised error messages, without having to write 3 individual tests. By writing the test routine once. we can call it as many times as we wish, creating a more intelligent script, at very little expense to the programmer. Perl programmers will recognise this as being similar to the die command in Perl.

As a third approach, we shall look at a simpler and cruder method. I tend to use this for building Linux kernels - simple automations which, if they go well, should just get on with it, but when things go wrong, tend to require the operator to do something intelligent (ie, that which a script cannot do!):

```
#!/bin/sh
cd /usr/src/linux && \
    make dep && make bzImage && make modules && \
    make modules_install && \
    cp arch/i386/boot/bzImage /boot/my-new-kernel && \
    cp System.map /boot && \
    echo "Your new kernel awaits, m'lord."
```

This script runs through the various tasks involved in building a Linux kernel (which can take quite a while), and uses the && operator to check for success. To do this with if would involve:

```
#!/bin/sh
cd /usr/src/linux
if [ "$?" -eq "0" ]; then
  make dep
    if [ "$?" -eq "0" ]; then
      make bzImage
      if [ "$?" -eq "0" ]; then
        make modules
        if [ "$?" -eq "0" ]; then
          make modules_install
          if [ "$?" -eq "0" ]; then
            cp arch/i386/boot/bzImage /boot/my-new-kernel
            if [ "$?" -eq "0" ]; then
              cp System.map /boot/
              if [ "$?" -eq "0" ]; then
                echo "Your new kernel awaits, m'lord."
              fi
            fi
          fi
        fi
      fi
    fi
  fi
fi
```

```
fi
```

... which I, personally, find pretty difficult to follow.

The && and || operators are the shell's equivalent of AND and OR tests. These can be thrown together as above, or:

```
#!/bin/sh
cp /foo /bar && echo Success || echo Failed
```

This code will either echo

```
Success
```

or

```
Failed
```

depending on whether or not the cp command was successful. Look carefully at this; the construct is:

```
command && command-to-execute-on-success \
   || command-to-execute-on-failure
```

Only one command can be in each part. This method is handy for simple success / fail scenarios, but if you want to check on the status of the echo commands themselves, it is easy to quickly become confused about which && and || applies to which command. It is also very difficult to maintain. Therefore this construct is only recommended for simple sequencing of commands.

In earlier versions, I had suggested that you can use a subshell to execute multiple commands depending on whether the cp command succeeded or failed:

```
cp /foo /bar && \
   ( echo Success ; echo Success part II; ) || \
   ( echo Failed ; echo Failed part II )
```

But in fact, Marcel found that this does not work properly. The syntax for a subshell is:

```
( command1 ; command2; command3 )
```

The return code of the subshell is the return code of the final command (`command3` in this example). That return code will affect the overall command. So the output of this script:

```
cp /foo /bar && \
  ( echo Success ; echo Success part II; /bin/false ) ||\
  ( echo Failed ; echo Failed part II )
```

Is that it runs the Success part (because `cp` succeeded, and then - because `/bin/false` returns failure, it also executes the Failure part:

```
Success
Success part II
Failed
Failed part II
```

So if you need to execute multiple commands as a result of the status of some other condition, it is better (and much clearer) to use the standard `if`, `then`, `else` syntax.

Simple Expect Replacement

Here is a simple replacement for expect. A number of people have asked how this is done, and inspired by Sun's example I showed in Hints and Tips which is used in Sun Microsystems' Explorer utility, here is a very simple version of expect[27].

The syntax of `expect.txt` is very simple:

> S command E[delay] expected_text

So a command is marked by starting with "S" (for Send), and the expected result is marked with "E". Since some commands can take a while to complete, it is possible to specify a delay before expecting the result: "E10 $" will wait for 10 seconds before expecting a dollar prompt. If the expected text is not found, the script will wait one second, try again, then wait two seconds, then

---

27 http://www.nist.gov/el/msid/expect.cfm

three seconds, until either the expected text is found, or it hits a maximum - as defined by MAX_WAITS. The delay is optional, so "E $" will expect a prompt immediately.

Note that if MAX_WAITS=5, the maximum delay will not be five, but 1+2+3+4+5=fifteen seconds.

```
#!/bin/sh
# expect.sh | telnet > file1
host=127.0.0.1
port=23
file=file1
MAX_WAITS=5

echo open ${host} ${port}

while read l
do
  c=`echo ${l}|cut -c1`
  if [ "${c}" = "E" ]; then
    expected=`echo ${l}|cut -d" " -f2-`
    delay=`echo ${l}|cut -d" " -f1|cut -c2-`
    if [ -z "${delay}" ]; then
      sleep ${delay}
    fi
    res=1
    i=0
    while [ "${res}" -ne "0" ]
    do
      tail -1 "${file}" 2>/dev/null | grep "${expected}"
> /dev/null
      res=$?
      sleep $i
      i=`expr $i + 1`
      if [ "${i}" -gt "${MAX_WAITS}" ]; then
        echo "ERROR : Waiting for ${expected}" >> ${file}
        exit 1
      fi
    done
  else
    echo ${l} |cut -d" " -f2-
  fi
done < expect.txt
```

This is run as so:

```
$ expect.sh | telnet > file1
```

This will create a file, file1, which contains a transcript of the session. In this case, that will be the login process, an ls of /tmp, and the output of cal. For example:

```
telnet> Trying 127.0.0.1...
Connected to 127.0.0.1.
Escape character is '^]'.

declan login: steve
Password:
Last login: Thu May 30 23:52:50 +0100 2002 on pts/3 from localhost.
No mail.
steve:~$ ls /tmp
API.txt                cgihtml-1.69.tar.gz      orbit-root
cal
a.txt                  cmd.txt                  orbit-steve
apache_1.3.23.tar.gz   defaults.cgi             parser.c
b.txt                  diary.c                  patchdiag.xref
background.jpg         drops.jpg                sh-thd-1013541438
blocks.jpg             fortune-mod-9708.tar.gz  stone-dark.jpg
blue3.jpg              grey2.jpg                water.jpg
c.txt                  jpsock.131.1249
steve:~$ cal
      May 2002
Su Mo Tu We Th Fr Sa
          1  2  3  4
 5  6  7  8  9 10 11
12 13 14 15 16 17 18
19 20 21 22 23 24 25
26 27 28 29 30 31

steve:~$ exit
logout
```

Trap

Trap is a simple, but very useful utility. If your script creates temporary files, such as this simple script which replaces FOO for BAR in all files in the current directory, /tmp is clean when the script exits. If it gets interrupted partway through, though, there could be a file lying around in /tmp:

```sh
#!/bin/sh

trap cleanup 1 2 3 6

cleanup()
{
  echo "Caught Signal ... cleaning up."
  rm -rf /tmp/temp_*.$$
  echo "Done cleanup ... quitting."
  exit 1
}

### main script
for i in *
do
  sed s/FOO/BAR/g $i > /tmp/temp_${i}.$$ && mv
/tmp/temp_${i}.$$ $i
done
```

The `trap` statement tells the script to run `cleanup()` on signals 1, 2, 3 or 6. The most common one (CTRL-C) is signal 2 (SIGINT). This can also be used for quite interesting purposes:

```sh
#!/bin/sh

trap 'increment' 2

increment()
{
  echo "Caught SIGINT ..."
  X=`expr ${X} + 500`
  if [ "${X}" -gt "2000" ]
  then
    echo "Okay, I'll quit ..."
    exit 1
  fi
}

### main script
X=0
while :
do
  echo "X=$X"
  X=`expr ${X} + 1`
```

```
    sleep 1
done
```

The above script is quite fun - it catches a CTRL-C, doesn't exit, but just changes how it's running. How this could be useful for positive and negative effect is left as an exercise to the reader:) This particular example concedes to quit after 4 interrupts (or 2000 seconds). Note that anything will be killed by a `kill -9` `<PID>` without getting the chance to process it.

Here is a table of some of the common interrupts:

Number	SIG	Meaning
0	0	On exit from shell
1	SIGHUP	Clean tidyup
2	SIGINT	Interrupt
3	SIGQUIT	Quit
6	SIGABRT	Abort
9	SIGKILL	Die Now (cannot be trap'ped)
14	SIGALRM	Alarm Clock
15	SIGTERM	Terminate

Note that if your script was started in an environment which itself was ignoring signals (for example, under nohup control), the script will also ignore those signals.

echo : -n vs \c

As you may have noticed by now, when you use the echo statement, a newline is added at the end of the command. There is a fix for this ... well, more accurately, there are two fixes for this.

Some Unix systems use echo -n message to tell echo not to

append a newline; others use echo message \c to do the same thing:

```
echo -n "Enter your name:"
read name
echo "Hello, $name"
```

This will work on some systems, and will look like this:

```
Enter your name: Steve
Hello, Steve
```

However, on other systems, you need to write the code like this:

```
echo "Enter your name: \c"
read name
echo "Hello, $name"
```

Which will provide the same results for those systems.

Well, that's a pain. Here's a workaround which will work on both:

```
        if [ "`echo -n`" = "-n" ]; then
                n=""
                c="\c"
        else
                n="-n"
                c=""
        fi

  echo $n Enter your name: $c
  read name
  echo "Hello, $name"
```

If echo -n wasn't interpreted properly, it would just echo out the text -n, in which case, $n is set to the empty string, and $c is set to \c. Otherwise, the opposite is done, so $n is set to -n, and $c is set to the empty string.

We have already shown above a use of the simple but effective cut command. We shall discuss a few examples here some of the more common external programs to be used.

grep is an extremely useful utility for the shell script programmer. An example of grep would be:

```
#!/bin/sh
steves=`grep -i steve /etc/passwd | cut -d: -f1`
echo "All users with the word \"steve\" in their passwd"
echo "Entries are: $steves"
```

This script looks fine if there's only one match. However, if there are two lines in /etc/passwd with the word "steve" in them, then the interactive shell will display:

```
$> grep -i steve /etc/passwd
steve:x:5062:509:Steve Parker:/home/steve:/bin/bash
fred:x:5068:512:Fred Stevens:/home/fred:/bin/bash
$> grep -i steve /etc/passwd |cut -d: -f1
steve
fred
```

But the script will display:

```
Entries are: steve fred
```

By putting the result into a variable we have changed the NEWLINEs into spaces; the sh manpage tells us that the first character in $IFS will be used for this purpose. IFS is <space><tab><cr> by default. Maybe though we wanted to keep the NEWLINEs: It could look better if we made the spaces into NEWLINEs.... This is a job for tr:

```
#!/bin/sh
steves=`grep -i steve /etc/passwd | cut -d: -f1`
echo "All users with the word \"steve\" in their passwd"
echo "Entries are: "
echo "$steves" | tr ' ' '\012'
```

Note that tr translated the spaces into octal character 012
(NEWLINE). Another common use of tr is its use of range... it can
convert text to upper or lower case, for example:

```
#!/bin/sh
steves=`grep -i steve /etc/passwd | cut -d: -f1`
echo "All users with the word \"steve\" in their passwd"
echo "Entries are: "
echo "$steves" | tr ' ' '\012' | tr '[a-z]' '[A-Z]'
```

Here we have added a translation of [a-z] to [A-Z]. Note that
there are exactly the same number of values in the range a-z as A-
Z. This can then translate any character falling into the ASCII
range a-z into A-Z ... in other words, converting lowercase letters
into uppercase. tr is actually cleverer than this: tr [:lower:]
[:upper:] would do the job just as well, and possibly more
readably. It's also not as portable; not every tr can do this.

Cheating

Those who can't ... cheat

There is nothing wrong with cheating! Some things the shell just
isn't very good at. Two useful tools are sed and awk. Whilst these
are two hugely powerful utilities, which can be used as mini-
programming languages in their own right, they are often used in

```
```

shell scripts for very simple, specific reasons.

Whilst this means that the system has to load a largeish executable (52k for sed and 110k for awk), which is a nasty thing to do, the reason a good workman doesn't blame his tools, is that a good workman uses the *right* tools in the first place. So let me introduce these two, with very simple uses.

Cheating with awk

Consider wc, which counts the number of characters, lines, and words in a text file. Its output is:

```
$ wc hex2env.c
      102      189     2306    hex2env.c
```

If we want to get the number of lines into a variable, simply using:

```
NO_LINES=`wc -l file`
```

which would read in the whole line. Because the output is space-padded, we can't reliably get the number 102 into the string. Instead, we use the fact that awk works similarly to scanf in C - it strips unwanted whitespace. It puts these into variables $1 $2 $3 etc. So we use this construct:

```
NO_LINES=`wc -l file | awk '{ print $1 }'`
```

The variable NO_LINES is now 102.

Cheating with sed

Another handy utility is sed - the *stream editor*. Perl is very good at dealing with regular expressions, the shell isn't. So we can quickly use the s/from/to/g construct by invoking sed.For example:

```
sed s/eth0/eth1/g file1 > file2
```

changes every instance of `eth0` in file1 to `eth1` in file2. If we were only changing a single character, `tr` would be the tool to use, being smaller and therefore faster to load. Another thing that `tr` can't do, is remove characters from a file:

```
echo ${SOMETHING} | sed s/"bad word"//g
```

This removes the phrase "bad word" from the variable `${SOMETHING}`. It may be tempting to say, "But `grep` can do that!" - `grep` only deals with whole lines. Consider the file:

```
This line is okay.
This line contains a bad word. Treat with care.
This line is fine, too.
```

`grep` would remove the whole second line, leaving only a two-line file; `sed` would change the file to read:

```
This line is okay.
This line contains a . Treat with care.
This line is fine, too.
```

Telnet hint

This is a useful technique that I picked up from Sun's Explorer utility. Although telnet is not used on servers any longer, it is still used by some network devices, such as terminal concentrators and the like. By creating a script such as this, your own script, or from a command line, you can run:

```
$ ./telnet1.sh | telnet
```

I have had a few people ask me about this, and have tended to point them towards the expect suite of code, which is pretty complex and bulky; this code should be pretty portable amongst systems (so long as they've got egrep). If it doesn't work on your system, try using GNU grep with the -q switch, or a proprietary grep and direct to /dev/null. Still a lot easier than installing expect, though.

telnet1.sh[28]

```
#!/bin/sh
host=127.0.0.1
port=23
login=steve
passwd=hellothere
cmd="ls /tmp"

echo open ${host} ${port}
sleep 1
echo ${login}
sleep 1
echo ${passwd}
sleep 1
echo ${cmd}
sleep 1
echo exit
```

However, Sun add some clever error-checking code (note that the variables you could set and export from your current shell or shell script, to avoid storing passwords in readable files):

```
$ ./telnet2.sh | telnet > file1
```

28 https://www.shellscript.sh/eg/telnet1.txt

telnet2.sh[29]

```sh
#!/bin/sh
# telnet2.sh | telnet > FILE1
host=127.0.0.1
port=23
login=steve
passwd=hellothere
cmd="ls /tmp"
timeout=3
file=file1
prompt="$"

echo open ${host} ${port}
sleep 1
tout=${timeout}
while [ "${tout}" -ge 0 ]
do
    if tail -1 "${file}" 2>/dev/null | \
      egrep -e "login:" > /dev/null
    then
        echo "${login}"
        sleep 1
        tout=-5
        continue
    else
        sleep 1
        tout=`expr ${tout} - 1`
    fi
done

if [ "${tout}" -ne "-5" ]; then
  exit 1
fi

tout=${timeout}
while [ "${tout}" -ge 0 ]
do
    if tail -1 "${file}" 2>/dev/null | \
        egrep -e "Password:" > /dev/null
    then
        echo "${passwd}"
```

---

29 https://www.shellscript.sh/eg/telnet2.txt

```
          sleep 1
          tout=-5
          continue
     else
       if tail -1 "${file}" 2>/dev/null | \
       egrep -e "${prompt}" > /dev/null
       then
          tout=-5
       else
          sleep 1
          tout=`expr ${tout} - 1`
       fi
     fi
done

if [ "${tout}" -ne "-5" ]; then
   exit 1
fi

> ${file}

echo ${cmd}
sleep 1
echo exit
```

Note that with this version, the output is grabbed to file1, and that this file is actually used by the script to check on its progress. I have added "> ${file}" so that the output received into the file is just the output of the command, not the logging-in process too.

#!/ch/15

15. Quick Reference

This is a quick reference guide to the meaning of some of the less easily guessed commands and codes.

Command / Variable / Syntax Structure	Description	Example
&	Run the previous command in the background	`ls &`
&&	Logical AND	`if [ "$foo" -ge "0" ] && [ "$foo" -le "9"]`
||	Logical OR	`if [ "$foo" -lt "0" ] \|\| [ "$foo" -gt "9" ]` (not in Bourne shell)
^	Start of line	`grep "^foo"`
$	End of line	`grep "foo$"`
=	String equality (cf. -eq)	`if [ "$foo" = "bar" ]`

Command / Variable / Syntax Structure	Description	Example
!	Logical NOT	`if [ "$foo" != "bar" ]`
$$	PID of current shell	`echo "my PID = $$"`
$!	PID of last background command	`ls & echo "PID of ls = $!"`
$?	exit status of last command	`ls ;` `echo "ls returned code $?"`
$0	Name of current command (as called)	`echo "I am $0"`
$1	Name of current command's first parameter	`echo "My first argument is $1"`
$9	Name of current command's ninth parameter	`echo "My ninth argument is $9"`
$@	All of current command's parameters (preserving whitespace and	`echo "My arguments are $@"`

Command / Variable / Syntax Structure	Description	Example
	quoting)	
$*	All of current command's parameters (not preserving whitespace and quoting)	echo "My arguments are $*"
-eq	Numeric Equality	if ["$foo" -eq "9"]
-ne	Numeric Inquality	if ["$foo" -ne "9"]
-lt	Less Than	if ["$foo" -lt "9"]
-le	Less Than or Equal	if ["$foo" -le "9"]
-gt	Greater Than	if ["$foo" -gt "9"]
-ge	Greater Than or Equal	if ["$foo" -ge "9"]
-z	String is zero length	if [-z "$foo"]
-n	String is not zero	if [-n "$foo"]

Command / Variable / Syntax Structure	Description	Example
	length	
-nt	Newer Than	`if [ "$filea" -nt "$fileb" ]`
-d	Is a Directory	`if [ -d /bin ]`
-f	Is a File	`if [ -f /bin/ls ]`
-r	Is a readable file	`if [ -r /bin/ls ]`
-w	Is a writable file	`if [ -w /bin/ls ]`
-x	Is an executable file	`if [ -x /bin/ls ]`
parenthesis: (...)	Function definition	`function myfunc() { echo hello }`

#!/ch/16

16. Interactive Shell

Here are a few quick hints for using the UNIX or Linux shell interactively. Personally I recommend the bash shell for most interactive use; it is available on just about every *nix flavour, and very pleasant to use as a login shell. However the root shell should always be /bin/sh, whether that points to bash or Bourne shell.

bash

bash has some very handy history-searching tools; the up and down arrow keys will scroll through the history of previous commands. More usefully, Ctrl+r will do a reverse-search, matching any part of the command line. Hit ESC and the selected command will be pasted into the current shell for you to edit as required.

If you want to repeat a command you ran before, and you know what characters it started with, you can do this:

```
bash$ ls /tmp
(list of files in /tmp)
bash$ touch /tmp/foo
bash$ !l
ls /tmp
(list of files in /tmp, now including /tmp/foo)
```

As well as the arrow keys, you can use PageUp and PageDn to

navigate to the start and end of the command line.

ksh

You can make ksh more usable by adding history commands, either in vi or emacs mode. There are a number of ways to do this, depending on the exact circumstances. set -o vi, ksh -o vi, or exec ksh -o vi (where "vi" could be replaced by "emacs" if you prefer emacs mode).

If you want to start a ksh session from another interactive shell, you can just call ksh like this:

```
csh% # oh no, it's csh!
csh% ksh
ksh$ # phew, that's better
ksh$ # do some stuff under ksh
ksh$ # then leave it back at the csh prompt:
ksh$ exit
csh%
```

This will start a new ksh session, which you can exit from and return to the previous shell. Alternatively, you could replace the csh (or whatever shell) with a ksh shell, with the exec command:

```
csh% # oh no, it's csh!
csh% exec ksh
ksh$ # do some stuff under ksh
ksh$ exit

login:
```

The difference here is that you don't get the csh session back.

The good stuff is the history:

```
csh% ksh
ksh$ set -o vi
ksh$ # You can now edit the history with vi-like
```

```
commands,
 # and use ESC-k to access the history.
```

If you hit ESC then k, then by repeatedly hitting k you scroll backwards through the command history. You can use vi command-mode and entry-mode commands to edit the commands, like this:

```
ksh$ touch foo
 ESC-k (enter vi mode, brings up the previous command)
 w (skip to the next word, to go from "touch" to "foo"
 cw (change word) bar (change "foo" to "bar")
ksh$ touch bar
```

#!/ch/17

17. Exercises

Just a quick exercise I think might be useful in working out how good you are at shell scripting...

- Address Book
- Directory Traversal

Addressbook

Okay, it's boring, but here's your exercise for today: Create an addressbook program using the bourne or bourne-again shell. It should use functions to perform the required tasks. It should be menu-based, allowing you the options of:

- Search address book
- Add entries
- Remove / edit entries

You will also need a "display" function to display a record or records when selected.

Search

When the user searches for "Smith", the script should identify and display all "Smith" records. It is up to you whether this search is in

Surname only, or in the entire record.

Add

Input the data (Name, Surname, Email, Phone, etc). If it appears to be a duplicate, for bonus points offer to edit the existing record. Save the record into the data file when the user confirms.

Remove

Enter search criteria, narrow it down to one, confirm, then remove that record.

Edit

As remove, but use the existing record for default entries. For example, if you change the phone number, the session may look like this, if you only want to change John Smith's Phone Number:

```
Name  [ John Smith ]
Phone [ 12345 ] 54321
Email [ joe@smith.org.uk ]
```

Remove the old record, and add the new one. Alternatively, edit the existing record, though this may be more difficult.

Bonus Points

- Allow for cancel options (use "special" entries (^d, CR, ^c, etc))
- Add "Confirm" option.

Shell Scripting Tutorial

- Offer interactive / non-interactive modes. (ie, a menu-based version and a command-line (CLI)-based option.
- Play with getopt for CLI version.

Hints / Things to think about

- Suggested record format: Use colons to separate fields. John Smith: 54321:john@smith.example.com
- That way you can use "cut -d:" to read fields.
- Think about using IFS as an alternative to this method.
- Think about using space (" ") to separate fields, and convert any spaces in the input to underscores ("_") then convert them back again for display.

One answer I came up with is below; don't read unless you're stuck! Main file:
https://www.shellscript.sh/eg/addressbook/addr.sh.txt
Library file:
https://www.shellscript.sh/eg/addressbook/addr_libs.sh.txt

Directory Traversal

Create a shell script to traverse through a filesystem tree.

Example answers here:

https://www.shellscript.sh/eg/directories

Links To Other Resources

These are just a few of many other useful resources which can be found on the internet:

Steve Bourne's Introduction to the Unix Shell.
https://www.shellscript.sh/bourne.shtml

A pretty definitive document on quoting and escape characters
http://www.mpi-inf.mpg.de/departments/rg1/teaching/unixffb-ss98/quoting-guide.html

What to watch out for when writing portable shell scripts.
http://archive09.linux.com/articles/34658

The Rosetta Stone for Unix :
http://bhami.com/rosetta.html

Thank You!

Thank you for buying this book, and for reading it all the way to the end! I hope that you have found it useful, informative, and helpful.

The book depends on reviews to let potential readers know what they are getting. Please consider taking five seconds to give this ebook a star rating on Amazon, or even write a review - as long or short as you like, one sentence is fine, or a few paragraphs.

Things you might want to mention:

- Who this book is suitable for,
- Something you gained from the book,
- How did you find the writing style,
- Do you expect to revisit parts of the book in future,
- Was it a productive use of your time,

http://amzn.com/B00C2EGNSA – or just search Amazon for "Shell Scripting Tutorial"

The 600-Page Book

Steve Parker, the author of this tutorial, has also written a full book; Published by Wrox, the book "*Shell Scripting: Expert Recipes for Linux, Bash and more*" is available from all good retailers. ISBN 1118024486. RRP $49.99. Also available on Kindle:

http://steve-parker.org/book/ has the details; the book is available to buy online and in stores.

Steve Parker has also written "*How to Build a LAMP Server*", which details the installation of the LAMP stack, and building a working application on top of it, including MySQL configuration, phpMyAdmin use, and PHP development. This is currently only available on Amazon as an e-Book; search for "B00DAI6ATO", or for "How to Build a LAMP Server".

See http://steve-parker.org/publications/ for the latest information.

Made in the USA
San Bernardino, CA
10 October 2017